THE
FACTS
ABOUT

The Immune System

by Paul Almonte
and Theresa Desmond

Crestwood House
New York
Maxwell Macmillan Canada
Toronto
Maxwell Macmillan International
New York   Oxford   Singapore   Sydney

LIBRARY OF CONGRESS CATALOGING-IN-PUBLICATION DATA

Almonte, Paul.
    The immune system / by Paul Almonte and Theresa Desmond.—1st ed.
        p.   cm.—(Facts about)
    Includes index.
    Summary: Describes the human immune system and its workings.
    ISBN 0-89686-661-0
        1. Immune system—Juvenile literature.   2. Immunologic diseases—Juvenile
    literature. [1. Immune system.   2. Immunologic diseases.]   I. Desmond,
    Theresa.   II. Title.   III. Series: Facts about (Crestwood House)
    QR181.8.A46   1991
    616.07'9—dc20   91-11127
                                                                                      CIP
                                                                                       AC

PHOTO CREDITS

Cover: Jeff Greenberg
Jeff Greenberg: 4, 7, 8, 10, 13, 15, 17, 19, 21, 24, 30, 32–33, 38, 40–41.
Ned Matura: 23, 28–29, 42.
American Diabetes Association: 36–37.

CRESTWOOD HOUSE

Crestwood House
Macmillan Publishing Company
866 Third Avenue
New York, NY 10022

Maxwell Macmillan Canada, Inc.
1200 Eglinton Avenue East
Suite 200
Don Mills, Ontario M3C 3N1

Macmillan Publishing Company is part of the Maxwell Communication Group of Companies.

Printed in the United States of America

First edition

10   9   8   7   6   5   4   3   2   1

CONTENTS

INTRODUCTION

Visiting friends last weekend, 13-year-old Alice was excited to find out that their family cat had just given birth to four kittens. But after five minutes of playing with the tiny bundles of fur, Alice wasn't so excited anymore. Her eyelids were swollen, her nose was running, she was sneezing, and her hands and arms were itchy and red. Alice felt miserable. What's going on? she thought. Her friend's father noticed Alice's swollen eyes. He asked her if she had a cold. "I don't think so," said Alice confusedly. "Well, then," he said, "are you allergic to cats?" Allergic to cats? Alice looked down at the kittens. They mewed and looked back at her curiously. "Oh, no," she groaned, sneezing again.

Coming home from school yesterday, Martin noticed how tired he felt. His muscles ached. His throat was sore. His head felt heavy. After a couple of hours spent trying to do his homework, Martin's head was pounding, his eyes hurt, and his nose was running. There was no mistaking these feelings. Martin had the flu. He crawled into bed and called for his mother to bring the thermometer. "Great," he said. "This is just what I need! I have three big tests next week, and I get sick." His mother looked at him. Gently she put her hand on his forehead. "Give yourself a couple days' rest," she said. "You must have

Allergies to animals can cause swelling, itchy skin and sneezing.

caught a virus." Martin sighed. He had to admit, rest sounded pretty good.

Andrew sat in his favorite overstuffed chair, staring out the window. The 24-year-old man kept going over everything his doctor had just told him. He remembered the words. He wanted to forget the visit altogether. Should I really be surprised? he asked himself. He had suspected what the doctor's diagnosis would be. His weight loss, his tiredness and his diarrhea indicated that something was wrong. He knew what had happened to friends of his who had had similar symptoms. But actually hearing the words, "You have *AIDS*," made the disease so real, so scary. Now he had to face the full meaning of the disease. He knew he would die. But when? How? And how would he live from now on?

Alice, Martin and Andrew face very different situations. Alice's discomfort might last for a few hours. Martin will probably have to stay in bed for a few days and take some kind of medication. Andrew's situation is much more serious. He must confront a fatal disease. But in spite of the differences between allergies, the flu and AIDS, all are related to the same thing: the immune system.

Some illnesses require a visit to your doctor. Others will only make you feel uncomfortable for a few hours.

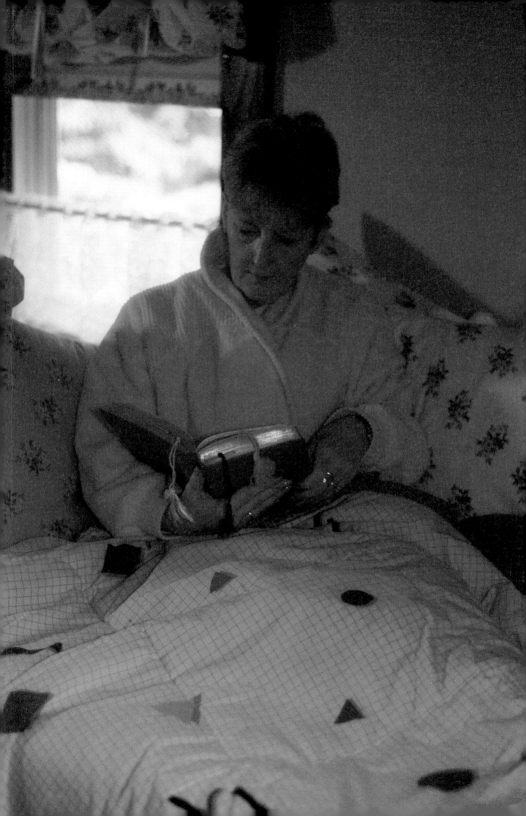

Each person's immune system is personalized. People respond to foreign agents in different ways.

WHAT IS THE IMMUNE SYSTEM?

The immune system is our internal defense system. It finds and destroys disease-causing agents that enter our bodies. The immune system is made up of thousands of different cells. Each one is highly specialized. When our bodies are attacked by a foreign substance, the appropriate immune cells go to work: They find the enemy cells and work to rid the body of them.

Each person's immune system is personalized. The enemy cells and the immune cells react to one another differently in every one of us. We will be looking at the role of the immune system in Alice's, Martin's and Andrew's cases. But first we need to know a little bit about how the immune system works.

Almost every cell has its own unique group of molecules that distinguishes it from other cells. The molecules are arranged in different ways on each cell. Some molecules, called *antigens*, have the ability to cause the immune system to respond.

Once the immune system is triggered, it has to distinguish between foreign antigens and the body's own antigens. The antigens of foreign cells are called *nonself*. Nonself antigens can include *viruses, bacteria,* chemicals, dust or certain foods. The body's own antigens are called *self*. When a person's immune system is functioning correctly, it distinguishes between self and nonself antigens and responds only to those it knows are harmful.

LYMPHOCYTES

The main component of the body's immune system is the *lymphocyte*. Lymphocytes are white blood cells produced in the liver, spleen and bone marrow (and a few other places). Their job is to identify and destroy foreign antigens.

There are two basic types of lymphocytes, *B cells* and

T cells. B cell lymphocytes grow in a person's bone marrow. There, they develop *receptors*. The receptors help the B cells recognize and react with antigens. T cells are lymphocytes that develop in the thymus gland, located in a person's chest. There are a few different kinds of T cells.

The T cells and B cells work together to attack nonself antigens. T cells are constantly traveling through the bloodstream. When virus cells enter the body, a group of T cells heads straight to the invaded area. Some of the group immediately begin fighting the nonself antigens. Sometimes those T cells alone can fight off the invader. At other times, many of those T cells are destroyed by the invading virus. But they have helped the body by slowing down the invading cells.

Other T cells, which have recognized the presence of nonself antigens, carry back a pattern of the enemy's molecular makeup to the appropriate B cell. The T cells need to show the B cells the exact pattern of the nonself antigen. It is as if they are looking for the right key to fit a lock. They first trace a pattern of the lock from the nonself antigen. Then they carry that pattern to the specific B cell that can attack the antigen.

The B cell then reproduces itself. It makes thousands of cells that have the enemy's antigen pattern. These are called *antibodies*. They are protein molecules that will ultimately destroy the nonself agents. The antibody is the "key" that is made from the pattern the T cell has carried to the B cell. The antibody key fits the invading antigen's lock and, by unlocking it, can destroy it.

Lymphocytes are the main component of the body's immune system. They are white blood cells.

Another group of T cells tells the body to speed up, or increase, antibody production. These are known as *helper T cells. Suppressor T cells* tell it to slow down or stop producing antibodies once the foreign substance has been destroyed.

Scientists often tell us to think of our immune system as an army that defends us against foreign invaders. Groups of T cells and B cells are like different troops. Each has a specialized job. When an invader enters our bodies, the troops are signaled to begin combat.

When the T cells recognize an invader, some of them begin attacking at the front line. Others hurry back to the B cell troops to tell them what specific weapons are needed. The B cells can produce weapons—antibodies that perfectly match the enemy's weapons. A minibattle then takes place within your body. Most of the time your immune system successfully defends you against invaders such as chemicals, bacteria or dust.

THE "BOY IN THE PLASTIC BUBBLE"

For most of us the immune system works amazingly well. Martin, for example, will suffer with the flu for a few days. As his lymphocytes identify and destroy the

Babies who are born without immune systems cannot even be held by their parents.

foreign antigens, he will gradually feel better. His immune system works quickly to heal his body. But in extremely rare cases, problems with the immune system can be life-threatening.

Two-year-old James seemed to be a normal child. He played in his crib. He smiled and cried. He loved seeing his parents. There was just one problem with him. And it was a big problem. James had no immune system. This meant that he had no protection from infections, viruses or any foreign substances that entered his body. Even the slightest germ would lead to a serious problem. His body could not produce antibodies to fight it.

Because of this James had to live in a special, germ-free environment. Everything had to be sterilized. James could not even be touched by human hands. His parents couldn't hold him. He had to be kept away from everything that could possibly lead to infection. Even the air he breathed had to be sterilized. And he would have to spend his whole life like this.

James suffered from *combined immunodeficiency disease*. It is extremely rare. Those who have it, like James, are born without B or T lymphocytes. Basically they have no immune system. They are so susceptible to disease that they must be kept in a totally sterilized environment. Unfortunately, an artificial defense system usually isn't as effective as the body's natural immune system. Most people with this disease die when they are very young.

The most famous case of this terrible disease involved a young boy named David. He was known as the "Boy in

A person who is allergic to pollen might not be able to enjoy a summer day without allergy medicine.

the Plastic Bubble." David lived nearly 12 years in a specially designed hospital room made almost germ-free. The room was a huge airtight plastic incubator. It came to be called a plastic bubble. It surrounded David completely but allowed him room to move around. No one could ever touch him. And he could not touch or eat anything that hadn't been specially treated. Eventually doctors attempted to build up David's immune system. They tried a variety of medicines. They hoped he would be able to live in a germ-free room in his home. But David died from a series of infections soon after his release from the hospital.

Since then doctors have begun trying bone marrow transplants to help people like David. The bone marrow is the place where immune cells are manufactured. Doctors hope that new bone marrow might be able to build up the patient's defense system.

THE OVERACTIVE IMMUNE SYSTEM

EMILY'S BEE STING

Most problems with the immune system are not as extreme as David's. However, they can still be life-threatening. Let's take a look at one such case.

Tarantulas carry a deadly venom. But for some people, a bee sting can be just as dangerous.

Fourteen-year-old Emily was happy to go to school on Tuesday. Her earth-science class was going on a field trip to the nearby state park. Emily was looking forward to examining all the flowers, rocks, insects and animals in the park's nature preserve.

Emily's class was being led around the preserve by a park ranger. The ranger knew the names of all the plants and animals they came across. But suddenly, while smelling a beautiful rose the ranger had pointed out, Emily was stung by a bee. Immediately she became frighteningly ill. Her eyes became puffy, and itchy bumps appeared all over her skin. It was hard for her to breathe and she felt faint. Luckily the park ranger recognized Emily's symptoms as those of a severe allergic shock. He quickly administered a drug called Adrenalin. This helped to lessen the attack so that Emily could be taken to a hospital for treatment.

Emily's allergic problem is called *anaphylactic shock*. It is a sudden overreaction of the body's immune system to a foreign substance like bee venom. Such reactions can also be caused by penicillin, horse serum and other types of medicine. Fortunately, Emily doesn't have to give up her love of the outdoors. She now carries a bee-sting kit with her. It contains medicine to help control her reactions.

People who are allergic to drugs like penicillin can get Medic Alert bracelets. They can wear these bracelets on their wrists. They tell doctors or emergency medical workers not to administer a particular drug because of the chance of violent allergic reaction.

Earlier we read about Alice's *allergic reaction* to cats.

Her immune system is unusually sensitive to certain foreign agents, like those from cat hair. When those nonself agents enter her body, her immune system treats them like dangerous agents and overreacts. Certain B cells begin producing more antibodies than are needed. Those cells then release a chemical substance called *histamine*. Once histamine is released, it causes intense itching and the release of fluids. This is why Alice's nose was running and her eyes and nose became itchy.

When a foreign agent enters our bodies, our B cells release a substance called histamine. Histamine makes our eyes itchy and our noses runny. Some allergy medicines are antihistamines. They help clear up these symptoms.

MR. ELLISON'S ARTHRITIS

Henry Ellison was in great pain. For many of his 48 years all the joints in his body ached. His knees, fingers and back all throbbed with a pain that would not go away. Now the pain was growing steadily worse. Henry could hardly straighten his fingers without crying out in agony. He had to go to a doctor to find out what was wrong and whether anything could be done. He made an appointment with his physician, Dr. Frieda Drieser, for the next week.

Dr. Drieser's examination revealed some bad news. Mr. Ellison had a disease called *rheumatoid arthritis.* It is a disease, the doctor explained, that attacks the tissue in a person's joints. It develops when a person's immune system mistakes regular body cells for foreign substances. When this happens, the immune system produces lymphocytes to destroy the cells. The tissue in Mr. Ellison's joints was being attacked by his own immune system. That was what was causing the pain and swelling. Unfortunately, Dr. Drieser said, there is no cure for this disease. However, doctors can give rheumatoid arthritis patients *immunosuppressive* drugs. These block the normal activity of the immune system. This treatment does not stop all the attacking antibodies. But it does lessen the pain they cause.

In diseases like rheumatoid arthritis, the immune system attacks the cells of normal, healthy organs and tis-

Doctors and researchers are hoping that they will soon be able to treat diseases such as diabetes with immunosuppressive drugs.

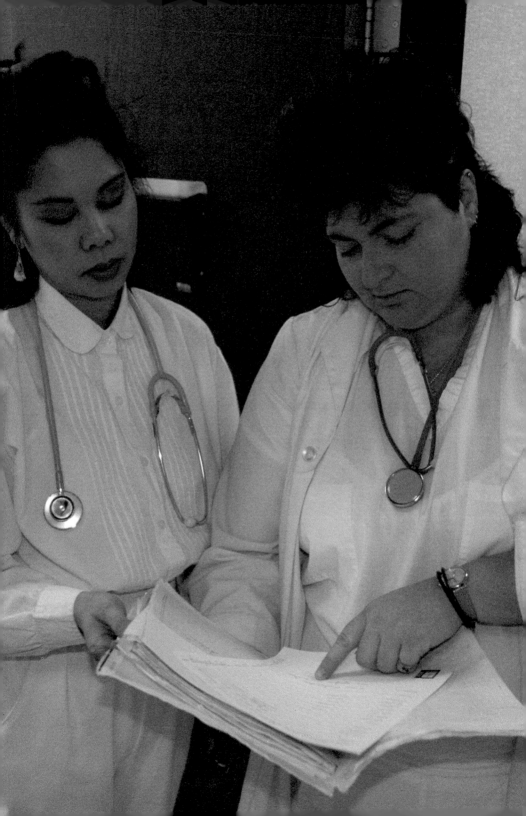

from a cowpox sore on a woman's hand. He did this to protect the boy from the more dangerous smallpox disease that was killing many people. Dr. Jenner had noticed that those people who got the mild cowpox infection were never struck by the then fatal smallpox disease.

Almost a hundred years later, a Frenchman named Louis Pasteur had a similar idea. He noticed that people who survived a dangerous disease, like rabies, were never severely troubled by it again. Pasteur's idea was to introduce a small amount of the disease into a person's body. His ultimate intention was to protect the person from a more serious attack.

Pasteur did this to a young boy named Joseph Meister. Joseph had been bitten by a rabid dog. Pasteur injected Joseph with a small dose of serum from a rabbit that had died of rabies. When Joseph survived the rabies attack, Pasteur realized his test had worked. The small dose of rabies had somehow protected Joseph from the more dangerous infection.

Only later did doctors learn the reason why Jenner's and Pasteur's vaccinations worked. About five years after Pasteur's discovery, a German scientist named Emil Behring found that immunity depends on certain molecules, or antibodies, found in a person's bloodstream. He discovered that the antibodies from one person could be injected into someone else. These antibodies could then protect the person from a particular poison, or toxin. Behring called these injected antibodies *antitoxins*.

In the 20th century, vaccines have been developed to help protect people from typhoid fever, polio and measles.

The use of antitoxins as a form of vaccination is called passive immunization. Its protection lasts only a few weeks. In contrast, active immunization provides protection for many years. In active immunization, a weakened form of the toxin or the foreign substance itself is injected into the person.

Normally, when infectious agents enter the body, antibodies are formed to destroy them. Some of the antibodies remain in the body after the infection is destroyed. Those antibodies remember the pattern of the antigen from the infectious agent. If the agent shows up again, the antibodies are already there to attack it.

Immunization works along with the body's natural immune system. When we immunize a person, a little bit of the infectious agent is purposely injected into that person. The body then forms antibodies to respond to the small dose of the foreign agent. Thus, if the disease-carrying agent ever strikes in full force, the body already has antibodies that can fight it.

In the early 20th century vaccines were developed for typhoid fever, whooping cough and tetanus, among other diseases. Vaccines for viral diseases such as polio and measles were found in the 1950s and 1960s. Today children in the United States and many other countries are vaccinated against these diseases as a matter of course.

THE IMMUNE SYSTEM AND ORGAN TRANSPLANTS

Walter is a 62-year-old man with a history of heart disease in his family. Ten years ago he suffered a mild heart attack. At his last physical examination, his doctor told him his heart disease had gotten worse. Years of smoking, poor eating habits, and a lack of exercise had overworked and weakened his heart. So Walter was not too surprised when his doctor suggested a heart transplant. He knew it would be serious surgery. His own heart would actually be removed, and another person's heart would be put in its place. Walter thought that once the surgery was completed successfully, his body would soon be back to normal.

But a couple of months after his heart transplant, Walter realized why his doctors had lectured him so often about the immune system. Walter's operation had been a success. But his body was having trouble getting used to the new heart. In fact, his body was doing everything it could to reject the new organ. Walter was taking many drugs to help his body readjust. Still, it was difficult to understand why his body would reject a new and improved heart.

Some immune system diseases are serious. They force people to come to terms with difficult situations.

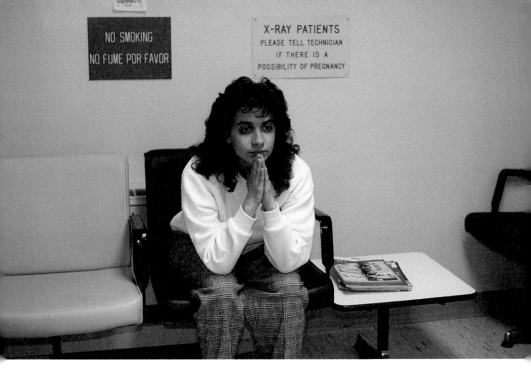

Most of the time, your immune system defends you against invaders like chemicals, bacteria and dust. But sometimes we need medical attention.

Because the immune system is so quick to react against substances foreign to the body, it creates problems for people who have organ transplants. When an organ, such as a heart, kidney or liver, is taken from a different person, the receiver's lymphocytes regard the new organ as foreign. The lymphocytes then begin to do their job. They attack this nonself substance.

The same process that helps to heal us by attacking foreign agents can also harm us by attacking a foreign organ that we need to live. Without some form of treatment, a transplanted organ would be destroyed within ten days. Fortunately, scientists have found ways to stop the

30

immune system from attacking transplants. They give the patient immunosuppressive drugs such as cyclosporine. These drugs stop the immune system from producing antibodies that could destroy the new organ.

Unfortunately, immunosuppressive treatment has some negative side effects. For one, an organ transplant patient, like Walter, must take these drugs for many years after the operation. If treatment is stopped, the immune system will again make antibodies to attack the organ. This is an annoying and dangerous problem. Also, immunosuppressive treatment weakens the entire immune system. It makes the patient more susceptible to viruses and infections. It forces the patient to take even more drugs to combat infections.

THE IMMUNE SYSTEM AND CANCER

We've all heard about the many types of cancer, such as breast cancer, skin cancer and lung cancer. But scientists still are not sure exactly how cancer starts in the body. They know that something happens to cause certain cells to act abnormally. Instead of performing their usual function and then dying, these cells suddenly change. They begin dividing and reproducing with greater speed. The body soon has groups, or tumors, of these sick cells,

Scientists believe that our immune systems are constantly destroying cancer cells in our bodies.

which can travel to other parts of the body where they can grow into new tumors.

Why doesn't the immune system attack these sick cells? We've seen that when the T cells detect a nonself invader, they move to the site and attack it. Scientists believe that the immune system does detect the change that takes place when normal cells become cancer cells. The system then moves to destroy the cancer cells. Sometimes, scientists believe, the immune system is successful. In fact, they think that normal cells are constantly turning into cancer cells and that the immune system generally destroys them.

But sometimes the immune system misses an abnormal cell. An abnormal cell either does not show the signs of being nonself, or it is able to hide those signs. Such a cell is able to divide and reproduce. The cancer can then develop. The immune system does continue to fight the cancer, and at times it is able to slow down the growth of the cancer.

THE IMMUNE SYSTEM AND AIDS

Earlier we met Andrew, a young man who had just found out he has AIDS. AIDS stands for Acquired Immune Deficiency Syndrome. It is the name scientists have given to a recently discovered disease for which there is no known cure. Andrew contracted a virus called *HIV* (human immunodeficiency virus), which attacks the body's immune system. It is this virus that sometimes causes AIDS.

The virus travels through the bloodstream. It seeks out and enters the cells of the immune system. There, it begins to produce more viruses, which attack immune system cells. Eventually, most of the body's T cells, which fight off disease and infection, are destroyed.

This makes the AIDS patient unable to fight infections and cancers. The patient doesn't have enough immune system T cells to make antibodies to fight even the weakest of infections. So a person with AIDS is much more likely to get all sorts of diseases. When people are said to have died of AIDS, they have actually died from some kind of infection, like pneumonia. Because HIV, or the AIDS virus, had weakened their immune system, they were not able to fight off the infection.

Scientists have found the AIDS virus in body fluids like blood, saliva, semen, tears and urine. They believe that the virus is transmitted through sexual contact or by direct entry into the bloodstream. Having sex with someone who has the AIDS virus can lead to an exchange of the virus through semen. A transfer of the virus can also occur through blood transfusions or by sharing unsterilized hypodermic needles.

The virus cannot be transmitted through casual contact, such as shaking hands. And not everyone who becomes infected with HIV will actually get AIDS. Scientists are not sure why.

Diseases and conditions that are related to the immune system can affect people of all ages and ethnic backgrounds.

However, scientists do know ways to protect ourselves from getting the AIDS virus. Practicing safe sex, which includes using condoms; testing blood-transfusion equipment; and avoiding contaminated needles can all help reduce the risk of acquiring AIDS.

CURRENT RESEARCH

Scientists and researchers are studying the immune system for ways to combat such diseases as heart disease, cancer and AIDS.

Recently some researchers have claimed that heart disease caused by hardening of the arteries is an autoimmune problem. They say that for some reason the body's immune system produces antibodies that attack the cells which carry away cholesterol. Without these cells, cholesterol is trapped in blood vessel walls. There, it hardens vessels and clogs arteries—causing heart attacks.

Scientists are also looking for ways to help the immune system fight cancer. They have learned that there are certain proteins in the body called *interferons*. These proteins interfere with the growth of cancer cells. Now scientists can make interferon in a laboratory. This means that larger doses of interferon are available to cancer patients. But too much interferon is also dangerous. So scientists are still working to find out how to use these helpful but powerful proteins. Researchers have many other ideas about how to fight cancer. They are even working on a

It's important to educate kids about AIDS and others diseases so that they know what they can do to stay healthy.

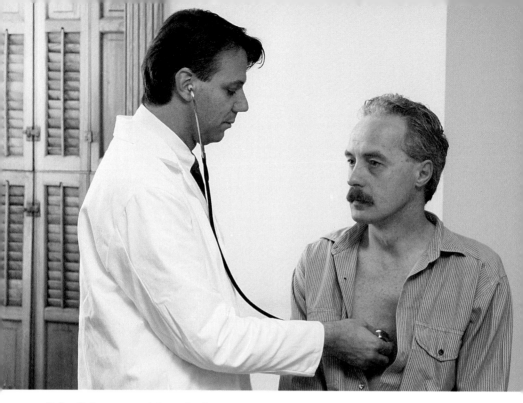

Scientists are studying the immune system to determine ways to combat heart disease, cancer and AIDS.

way to join cancer cells from mice with human cells to make special cancer-fighting antibodies.

The most immediate immune system research involves finding a cure for AIDS. Scientists still do not know how to destroy HIV. When they have tried to rebuild an AIDS patient's immune system, the virus just attacks it again. Researchers have begun to develop drugs to fight the virus. One drug called *AZT* helps AIDS patients by easing some of the symptoms of the disease. But the drug cannot cure AIDS or destroy the virus.

Scientists are now trying to develop a vaccine against HIV. The vaccine would work in the same way as other vaccines. Healthy people would be given a small amount of the virus's identifying antigen. Their immune systems would then be stimulated to produce the antibodies needed to destroy the HIV antigens. But the AIDS virus changes itself quickly. So it is difficult for the immune system to produce just the right antibodies to match the foreign antigens. It is as if the immune system finally learns which key, or antibody, should fit the lock. But the lock keeps changing.

FOR MORE INFORMATION

Your local library can help you find out more about the immune system. To learn more about AIDS, you can call or write to:

National AIDS Information Clearinghouse
P.O. Box 6003
Rockville, MD 20850
1-800-458-5231

GLOSSARY/INDEX

AIDS *(Acquired Immune Deficiency Syndrome)* 6, 34–44—*An infectious disease in which a virus, called HIV, attacks the helper T cells of the immune system.*

ALLERGIC REACTION 5, 16–19—*A situation in which the immune system overreacts to an antigen or other foreign substance.*

ANAPHYLACTIC SHOCK 18—*A sudden and severe body-wide allergic reaction that can be fatal.*

ANTIBODIES 11–12, 19–22, 25–26, 30–33, 39–43—*Protein molecules made by the body to help destroy foreign substances, or antigens, in the body.*

ANTIGENS 9–14, 26, 30, 43—*Substances that cause the immune system to produce antibodies. The antigens of foreign bodies such as viruses and bacteria are called **NON-SELF**. The body's own antigens are called **SELF**. A healthy person's immune system distinguishes between self and non-self antigens and responds only to those it knows are harmful.*

ANTITOXIN 25–26—*A substance that counteracts a specific toxin, or poison; an antibody used in immunization to combat an infectious disease.*

AUTOIMMUNE DISEASES 20–22—*Diseases that occur when the body's immune system attacks its own tissue as if it were a foreign substance.*

AZT 42—*Azidothymidine or Zidovudine, a drug which suppresses the reproduction of the human immunodeficiency virus, HIV, in the body. It is used to treat AIDS patients.*

B CELLS 9–14—*A type of white blood cell, or lymphocyte, that makes antibodies to fight infection.*

BACTERIA 9—*One-celled organisms that can cause infection.*

COMBINED IMMUNODEFICIENCY DISEASE 12–16—*A rare disease in which a person is born without T or B lymphocytes. This disease leaves the patient susceptible to infection from almost any foreign bacteria or virus.*

HISTAMINE 19—*A chemical the body releases during an allergic reaction. It causes runny noses and itchy eyes.*

HIV 35, 42–43—*Human Immunodeficiency Virus. A virus that attacks the body's immune system. It is this virus that causes AIDS.*

IMMUNIZATION 26—*Any medical procedure that enables a person to develop protection against specific disease-producing organisms.*

IMMUNOSUPPRESSION 20–22, 30–31—*The act of temporarily blocking the normal activities of the immune system, usually to prevent a transplanted organ from being* *rejected. Immunosuppressive drugs perform this function.*

INTERFERON 39—*Proteins made by the body that interfere with the growth of cancer cells. Interferon is also produced in the laboratory.*

LUPUS ERYTHEMATOSUS 22—*An autoimmune disease in which the immune system damages the tissue in the skin, blood vessels, heart and kidneys.*

LYMPHOCYTE 9–16, 30–31—*A type of white blood cell that is made in the bone marrow and is an important part of the immune system.*

MULTIPLE SCLEROSIS 22—*An autoimmune disease that destroys brain tissue and impairs the function of the nerves.*

RECEPTOR 11—*A protein molecule that helps activate B cells to respond to and resist foreign substances, or antigens.*

RHEUMATOID ARTHRITIS 20–22—*An autoimmune disorder in which cells of the immune system move into the tissue of the joints and destroy the tissue and bone.*

SERUM 23–26—*The clear, fluid part of blood that is left after a clot forms. Serum contains antibodies that the body uses to fight disease and toxins (poisons). When antibodies from one person are injected into someone else, they are called antitoxins.*

T CELLS 11–14, 34–35—*Lymphocytes that help to regulate the immune system.* **HELPER T CELLS** *speed up production of antibodies by the plasma cells.* **SUPPRESSOR T CELLS** *slow down the process after bacteria or viruses have been defeated.*

TYPE I DIABETES 22—*Diabetes that occurs in children. Diabetes is a disease in which the body has trouble making insulin, an important chemical that breaks down sugars to make energy for the body's cells.*

VACCINATION 23–26, 43—*The introduction of a modified virus to trigger the production of antibodies against possible attacks of a specific disease.*

VIRUSES 9, 14, 34–43—*Microorganisms, smaller than bacteria, that invade body cells and cause infection.*